JAMES BOND

DANNY PEARSON

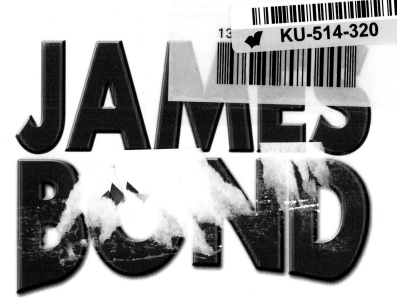

JB 007

100% UNOFFICIAL

WOW! facts

Badger Publishing Limited
Oldmedow Road,
Hardwick Industrial Estate,
King's Lynn PE30 4JJ
Telephone: 01438 791037

www.badgerlearning.co.uk

2 4 6 8 10 9 7 5 3 1

James Bond ISBN 978-1-78464-024-8

Publisher: Susan Ross
Senior Editor: Danny Pearson
Publishing Assistant: Claire Morgan
Designer: Fiona Grant
Series Consultant: Dee Reid

Photos: Cover Image: © nawson/Alamy
Page 5: © Keystone Pictures USA/Alamy
Page 6: © JHPhoto/Alamy
Page 8: © Pictorial Press Ltd/Alamy
Page 10: © AF archive/Alamy
Page 11: © AF archive/Alamy
Page 12: © Moviestore collection Ltd/Alamy
Page 13: © AF archive/Alamy
Page 14: © AF archive/Alamy
Page 17: © AF archive/Alamy
Page 18: © AF archive/Alamy
Page 19: c.Sony Pics/Everett/REX
Page 20: © United Archives GmbH/Alamy
Page 21: © Photos 12/Alamy
Page 24: © AF archive/Alamy
Page 25: © AF archive/Alamy
Page 26: © Photos 12/Alamy
Page 27: © Eddie Gerald/Alamy
Page 28: © Jeff Morgan 15/Alamy
Page 30: © Startraks Photo/REX

Attempts to contact all copyright holders have been made.
If any omitted would care to contact Badger Learning, we will be happy to make appropriate arrangements.

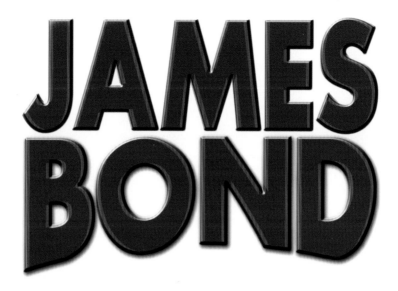

Contents

Vocabulary

anniversary	record-breaking
appeared	revolving
gyroplane	rickshaw
missions	supervillain

1. Bond... James Bond

All over the world, people know the name James Bond.

They might have read a book in which he is the hero. They have probably seen a James Bond film.

Ian Fleming was the creator of the Bond character and he wrote the first James Bond book, *Casino Royale*, in 1952.

WOW! facts
More than 100 million copies of the Bond books have been sold worldwide.

Where did Ian Fleming get his ideas for all the James Bond adventures?

During World War Two, Ian Fleming was in the British Special Forces.

He planned many dangerous missions to Germany to get information about their war plans.

After the war, when he began writing the James Bond books, those secret missions gave him lots of great ideas.

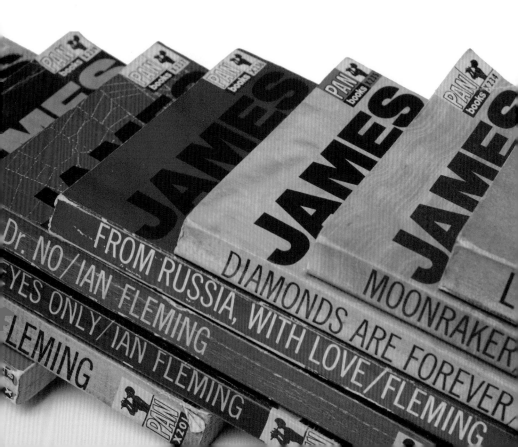

Ian Fleming wrote 14 Bond books in total.

They are:

Dr. No

Casino Royale

The Spy Who Loved Me

Goldfinger

Diamonds Are Forever

For Your Eyes Only

Moonraker

Octopussy/The Living Daylights

Live And Let Die

From Russia With Love

Thunderball

On Her Majesty's Secret Service

The Man With The Golden Gun

You Only Live Twice

Which films have you seen?

We find out from the books that when Bond was 11 years old, his mother and father died in a climbing accident. After that he had to live with his aunt.

When he grew up he worked for the British Secret Service.

They gave him the code name 007.

There have been six actors that have played James Bond on film.

Actor's name	Number of films
Sean Connery	6
George Lazenby	1
Roger Moore	7
Timothy Dalton	2
Pierce Brosnan	4
Daniel Craig	3

Daniel Craig is the first blond actor to play Bond.

2. The villains

The villains in the Bond films are almost as famous as Bond himself.

Not many villains appear in more than one Bond film (because James Bond has killed them at the end of the film) but Jaws is one who has.

He was famous for his size and his steel teeth.

WOW! facts

Richard Kiel, the actor who played Jaws, was over seven feet tall.

The supervillain, Scaramanga, appears in *The Man with the Golden Gun.*

Scaramanga is an assassin who charges $1 million per kill. He is such a good shot that his golden gun holds one bullet at a time.

He has a sidekick named Nick Nack who is less than four feet tall.

Goldfinger is another James Bond villain. He plans to attack Fort Knox in America where all the American gold is stored.

In one of the film's most famous scenes, Goldfinger has caught Bond and is about to kill him.

Bond is tied to a table and a laser beam is moving slowly towards him to cut him in half.

James Bond: *You expect me to talk?*
Goldfinger: *No Mr Bond, I expect you to die!*

Goldfinger's sidekick is Oddjob.

Oddjob wears a bowler hat that has a steel rim to it. He throws this hat at his enemies to kill them.

Ernst Stavro Blofeld is the Bond villain who has been in the most books and films. He is the head of a group called SPECTRE who want to take over the world.

In the films *From Russia with Love* and *Thunderball* we never see Blofeld's face.

We only see a close-up of his hands stroking his pet cat.

3. The cars

James Bond is famous for driving fast cars. The most famous of his cars is the Aston Martin DB5.

Features of James Bond's Aston Martin:
- revolving licence plates
- tyre slashers
- a bullet-proof shield
- machine guns
- ejector seat

WOW! facts

An Aston Martin used in one of the Bond films sold for over £2 million.

Other James Bond cars

Car	Top speed	Film
Lotus Esprit	135 mph	*The Spy Who Loved Me*

special features

It can change into a submarine
at the push of a button.
Cannons that spray cement.

Car	Top speed	Film
Aston Martin V12 Vanquish	190 mph	*Die Another Day*

special features

Is able to bend light and make the car invisible.
Front firing rockets.

Car	Top speed	Film
BMW Z3	115 mph	*Goldeneye*

Special feature

Stinger missiles behind the headlights.

James Bond doesn't only drive fast cars.
He has also driven:

- a tank through the streets of Russia in the film
  Goldeneye
- a Citroen 2CV in the film *For Your Eyes Only*
- a auto rickshaw in the film *Octopussy*
- a double-decker bus in the film *Live and Let Die*

The Bond films are full of record-breaking stunts.

In *Casino Royale*, stunt driver Adam Kirley, broke a world record. He flipped the Aston Martin DBS seven and three quarter turns during filming.

4. The gadgets

When Bond is on a mission he uses special gadgets given to him by the British Secret Service.

Q is the name of the man who gives Bond his cars and gadgets. The character Q was not in the original James Bond books but he has appeared in almost all of the Bond films.

WOW! facts

The actor Desmond Llewelyn has been in more Bond films than any other actor. He played Q in 17 films.

One of the strangest Bond gadgets was a submarine that looked like a crocodile. Bond used this to sneak into a floating palace.

A real crocodile was used for some of the scenes but it escaped under the film set at Pinewood studios in England.

It was found two weeks later!

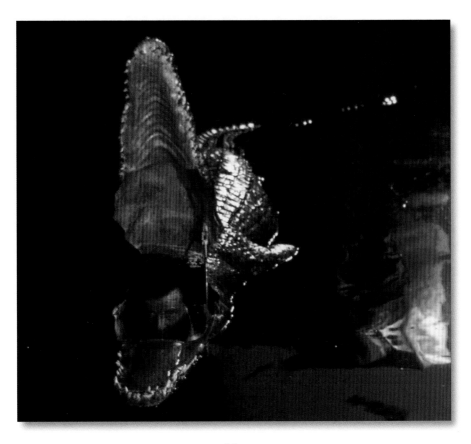

The gadgets given to James Bond by Q often save Bond's life:

- a Geiger counter to detect radioactivity
- a gun with a finger-print scanner so only Bond can fire it
- dynamite in a tube of toothpaste
- a bug detector in a phone

Many of the amazing gadgets seen in the early Bond films are now used in everyday life.

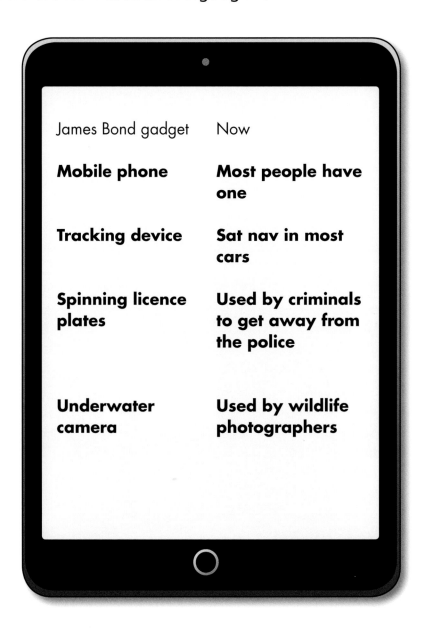

James Bond gadget	Now
Mobile phone	**Most people have one**
Tracking device	**Sat nav in most cars**
Spinning licence plates	**Used by criminals to get away from the police**
Underwater camera	**Used by wildlife photographers**

Below is James Bond's gyroplane. It is a mini one-man helicopter.

The amazing thing about it is it can be stored in four small cases.

James Bond uses it in the film *You Only Live Twice*.

The gyroplane has rocket launchers, machine guns and a flame thrower.

WOW! facts

Bond used a jet pack in the film *Thunderball* that was also used in the 1984 Olympic Games.

5. **From strength to strength**

The film *Skyfall* was released in 2012, which was the 50th anniversary of the first James Bond film.

Skyfall made more money at the box office than any other Bond film. It made over £620 million.

The Bond series is one of the most successful of all time and the films have made over £3 billion.

WOW! facts

A quarter of the world's population has seen at least one Bond film.

There are new Bond books being written all the time. Charlie Higson has written five Young Bond books.

Steve Cole has also written a Young Bond book, which came out in 2014.

These books for children have all the thrills, action, glamour and tension of the classic Bond books and films.

In 2012, Daniel Craig appeared with Queen Elizabeth II in a short film made for the London Olympics.

Two stunt doubles, dressed as the Queen and James Bond, parachuted out of a helicopter.

WOW! facts

The 86-year-old Queen was very happy to be a Bond girl.

The soundtracks for the Bond films are also very popular.

Some famous singers such as Tom Jones, Shirley Bassey and Madonna have all sung themes for Bond films.

Adele was the first to win an Oscar for her song *Skyfall*.

Questions

In what year did Ian Fleming write *Casino Royale*? *(page 5)*

How many Bond books did Ian Fleming write in total? *(page 7)*

What is the name of Scaramanga's sidekick? *(page 11)*

What does James Bond drive in the film *Goldeneye*? *(page 18)*

How many Bond films did Desmond Llewelyn appear in? *(page 20)*

What year was the 50th anniversary of the first James Bond film? *(page 26)*

Index